Disney

ALICE'S ADVENTURES

The Complete Visual Guide

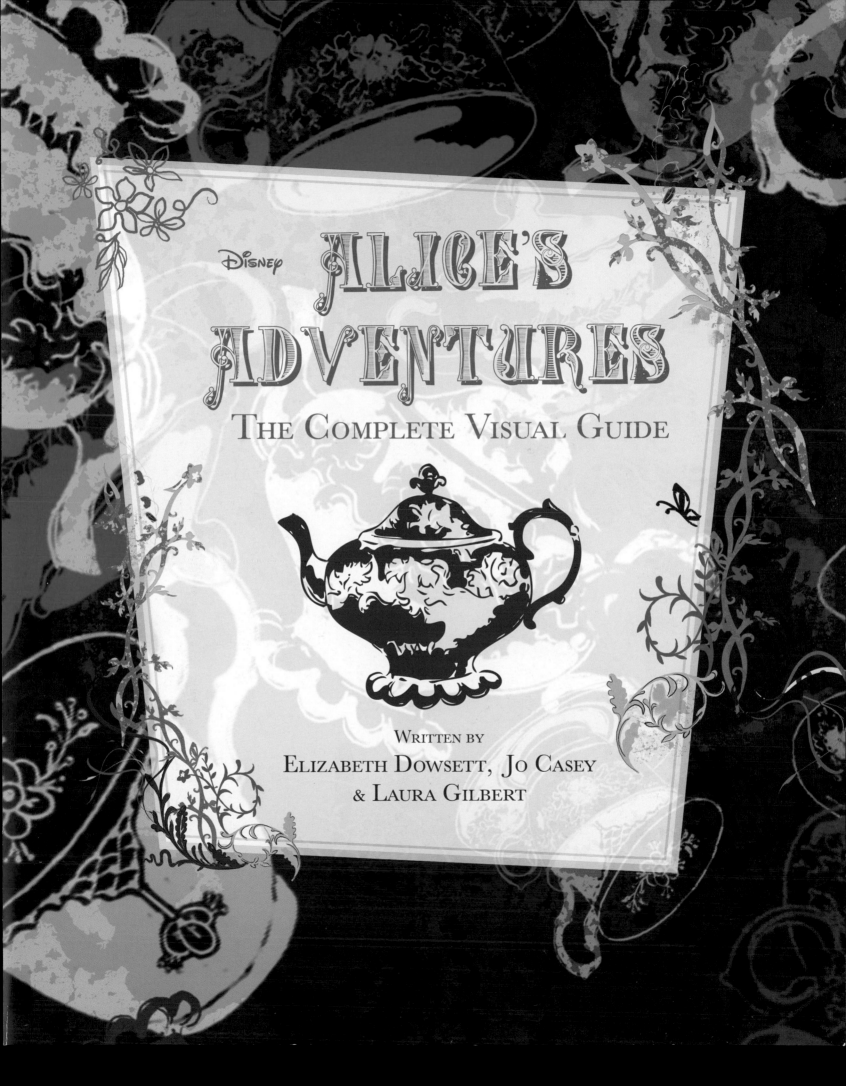

Disney ALICE'S ADVENTURES

THE COMPLETE VISUAL GUIDE

WRITTEN BY

ELIZABETH DOWSETT, JO CASEY
& LAURA GILBERT

CONTENTS

WELCOME TO UNDERLAND

THERE IS A PLACE like no place on Earth. A land full of wonder, mystery and danger. Some say to survive it you need to be as **mad as a hatter**, which, luckily, I am! Welcome to Underland!

I can guarantee that you will never have seen anywhere as **gallymoggers** as this place I call home. We've got everything here: a garden with Talking Flowers, a forest filled with mushrooms, the red desert of Crims and the muddy bogs of Gummer Slough.

And it's not just strange* places; the strangest things happen in Underland. Not that long ago the sky rained fish for no apparent reason, and when the gracious White Queen ruled over us, we would celebrate **Keltikidik**. This was a day when everyone wore white, drank milk and could only tell white lies.

What a **naughty Hatter!** I'm letting my memory run away with me. Memory... **mmmm**... that reminds me. I've been considering things that begin with the letter "m": moron, mutiny, murder, malice.... Where was I? Ah yes! Underland! It's bizarre, dangerous, absurd but oh so very beautiful. And if you get a teensy bit hungry, pop round to the March Hare's house for tea. There will be scones and cream and Battenburg cake and tea and.... Aargh! I'm late. The March Hare will be mad as a hatter. Oh no, that's me!

Fairfarren, my new friend. Enjoy your time in Underland. And remember – the impossible is possible. Just look around you.

Tarrant, the Mad Hatter

* "Strange" to you that is. To us Outlanders, this is as normal as can be!

ALICE IN WONDERLAND

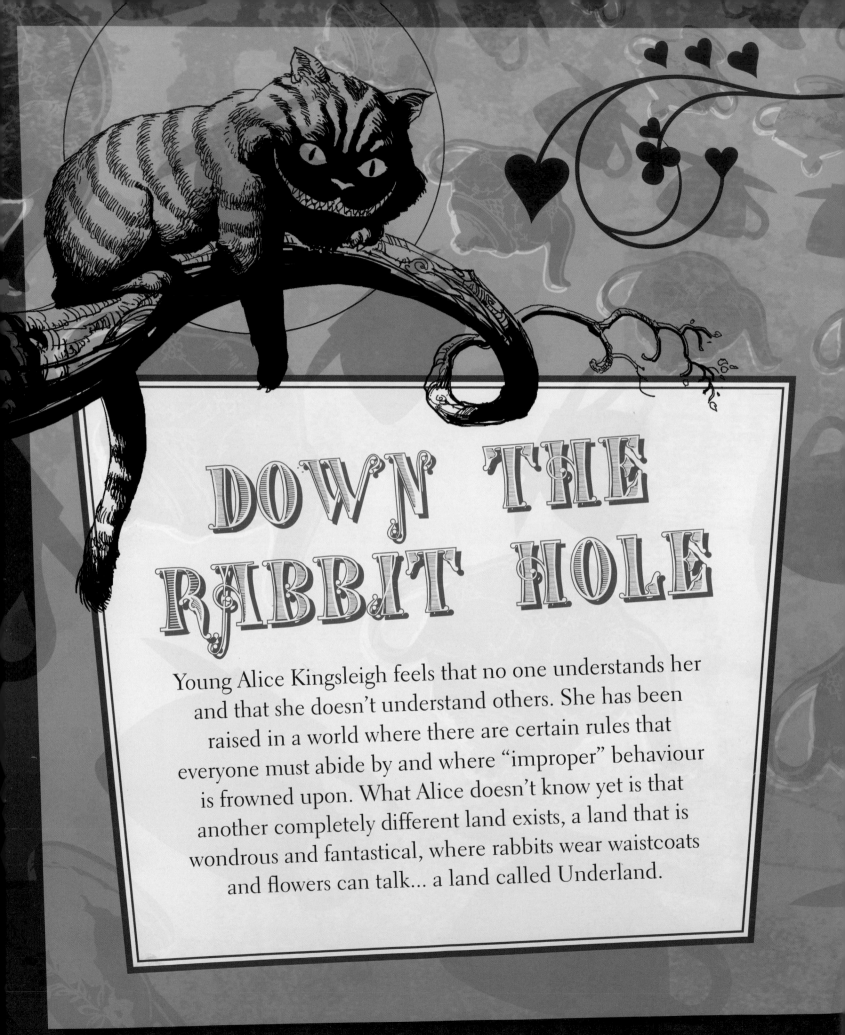

DOWN THE RABBIT HOLE

Young Alice Kingsleigh feels that no one understands her and that she doesn't understand others. She has been raised in a world where there are certain rules that everyone must abide by and where "improper" behaviour is frowned upon. What Alice doesn't know yet is that another completely different land exists, a land that is wondrous and fantastical, where rabbits wear waistcoats and flowers can talk... a land called Underland.

However, since the Horunvendush Day, Underland has been a gloomy, scary place to live. This was the day when the cruel Red Queen took control of Underland from her sister, the gentle White Queen. A group has formed that is opposed to the Red Queen called the Underland Underground Resistance. But the only way to free the people of Underland from the Red Queen's terrifying reign is to slay the Red Queen's fearsome Jabberwocky, using the Vorpal Sword. Rumour has it that there is only one person who can do this and save Underland. Her name is Alice Kingsleigh.

Join Alice on the biggest adventure of her life as she learns that anything is possible... and that dreams really do come true.

ALICE

Young Alice loved to play with her dolls and dress up in different costumes and hats. Her favourite hat was a black top hat.

ALICE KINGSLEIGH LIVES with her mother in London. Her father passed away when she was young and Alice has felt slightly out of place ever since. Now she is a young woman, she is trying to discover who she truly is. Never one to toe the line, Alice is confused by everyone telling her what is best for her. If only she could have a moment to work out what it is that *she* wants.

Daddy's Girl
Alice and her father, Charles, were very close. Alice sometimes feels that he was the only person who truly understood her. Charles taught Alice that anything was possible and that all the best people were mad as hatters!

"MY FATHER SAID HE SOMETIMES BELIEVED IN SIX IMPOSSIBLE THINGS BEFORE BREAKFAST."

Points of View
Alice loves her mother, Helen, very much, but she does not enjoy being told what to do by her. Helen prefers to do what is proper, whereas Alice thinks you should express yourself and do what you think is right.

The Thinker

Whether it is standing up for one of her beloved family or being honest when something doesn't make sense to her, Alice is not afraid to speak her mind. She also likes to be able to explain things rationally, but Alice will soon learn that not everything in life has a logical explanation.

Big Dream

Alice wants her independence and she is determined to get it. Everyone expects her to marry into the aristocracy and to stay close to home, but Alice wants more from her life. Maybe one day her dream will come true.

Alice has a curious recurring dream about a smiling cat, a rabbit in a waistcoat and a dodo with a walking stick. Her father tells her that it is only a dream and that dreams cannot harm her.

Alice's figure is not shaped by a corset, much to her mother's despair.

Delicate striped gloves add a touch of individuality to Alice's outfit.

Alice's dress is made out of blue silk and elegant lace.

13

ALICE'S FAMILY

EVERYONE IN ALICE'S family has an opinion on what Alice should do with her life, and they seem to have her whole future mapped out for her. But Alice sees the world differently to them. She misses her father, Charles, terribly – if he were here he would know exactly what she should do....

Charles Kingsleigh

Alice could always rely on her father to reassure her if she was having her bad dream. Alice and Charles were very similar and without him, she feels that there is no one like her in the world.

Charles Kingsleigh owned a trading company. His colleagues thought he had lost his senses when he wanted to expand his trading route to Asia. But Charles always believed that "the only way to achieve the impossible is to believe it is possible", a belief he has passed on to his daughter.

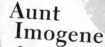

Aunt Imogene

Imogene is Alice's spinster aunt. She is waiting for her fiancé, a prince who cannot marry her unless he renounces his throne. It is a truly tragic tale but one that is entirely in Aunt Imogene's imagination. She'll be waiting a long time for her prince to come along....

Helen Kingsleigh

Alice's mother, Helen, has to bring up Alice alone after the death of her husband. She wants what is best for her daughter, but she sometimes struggles with Alice's stubborn and determined nature. She thinks that Alice won't get the best if she doesn't conform – not wearing stockings is not her idea of "proper" behaviour.

"WHO'S TO SAY WHAT IS PROPER?"

Margaret Manchester

Alice's sister, Margaret, believes that she has the perfect marriage with her husband, Lowell, and wants Alice to have the same. She tells Alice that Hamish Ascot, son of Lord and Lady Ascot, wants to marry her and it has all been arranged. After all, Alice can't do much better than a lord and, as Margaret reminds her, her pretty face won't last forever.

Lowell Manchester

Margaret's husband, Lowell, appears to be the perfect gentleman, and Margaret certainly believes so. However, Alice finds him partaking in some decidedly ungentlemanly behaviour – kissing a woman who isn't his wife! That is definitely not what Helen Kingsleigh would call "proper" behaviour.

15

ALICE'S ACQUAINTANCES

THE KINGSLEIGHS HAVE friends in high places. The noble Lord and Lady Ascot are even holding a summer party in Alice's honour – or that is what Alice thinks. Actually, it is a secret engagement party for Hamish and an unsuspecting Alice. But with the Chattaway sisters around, it won't be a secret for long!

Summer Party

Lord and Lady Ascot expect punctuality in all their guests. They have laid on a spectacular summer party with croquet, a string quartet and dancing. Only the best will do for their beloved son, Hamish.

Lord Ascot
Lord Ascot has bought Charles Kingsleigh's company. He was Charles' good friend and his only regret is that he didn't invest in Charles' venture to expand the business when Charles was alive.

Lady Ascot
Lady Ascot has been planning this engagement party for the last twenty years and anything less than perfect simply will not do. Her greatest fear in life is having ugly grandchildren, but she is sure that with Alice's good looks this won't happen.

Dancing

Alice finds dancing a quadrille with a strutting Hamish a bore. She would much rather imagine what it would be like to fly, but pompous Hamish thinks this is best kept to herself.

Alice and Hamish aren't the perfect match that everyone wants them to be. Alice has a vivid imagination, whereas practical Hamish believes daydreaming is an utter waste of time.

"AT LAST! WE THOUGHT YOU'D NEVER ARRIVE."

The Chattaways

Giggly and gossipy, Faith and Fiona Chattaway find it tough to keep a secret. They chat away so much, they can't help but let on to Alice that Hamish is going to propose to her!

In the gardens, Alice thinks she sees a rabbit dart past. Lady Ascot hates rabbits! This combined with the fact that her gardeners have planted the wrong colour roses leaves Lady Ascot annoyed. However, she manages to calm down enough to tell Alice that Hamish has a delicate digestion. Alice couldn't be less interested.

17

EAT ME, DRINK ME

WHEN ALICE SPIES a White Rabbit wearing a waistcoat, she wonders whether it is her turn to start believing in the impossible. Regardless, Alice thinks that a giant rabbit is far more interesting than a dull garden party and swiftly follows the bounding bunny.

Cascading blonde locks

Heading for a Fall

Alice loses sight of the White Rabbit until a paw grabs her and pulls her down a hole. As she plummets past crystal balls and human skulls, Alice thinks it odd that she thought her life was out of control before!

Sweet Dreams

Alice is used to bizarre dreams, but this is the oddest one yet! She keeps telling herself it is just a dream and considers pinching herself to wake up, but nothing works. Things are still very weird.

Alice's pretty dress wasn't made for tumbling down muddy rabbit holes.

Closed Doors

Alice lands in a Round Hall with lots of little doors. Each one is locked but there is a tiny key on top of a glass table. Alice tries the key in each door and finally finds the correct fit. Through the open door, Alice sees a beautiful – and strange – garden.

When a bottle of liquid, labelled with the words "Drink Me", appears on the table, curiosity makes Alice drink it. The liquid tastes vile, but it has a remarkable shrinking effect on Alice and she becomes small enough to fit through the door. However, the door is now locked and the key is atop the towering table!

This miniature cake, iced with the words "Eat Me", looks harmless, but Alice thought the same about the bottle of liquid!

All Grown Up

One bite of the cake and Alice shoots up, as quickly as she shrank. Thinking on her giant feet, she unlocks the door. She then drinks from the bottle to shrink herself, and walks through the door. Alice hopes she won't have to go through any more ups and downs.

"CURIOUSER AND CURIOUSER."

19

ROUND AND ROUND

The vast Round Hall at the end of the long rabbit hole is certainly
mysterious. The many doors are all different shapes and sizes, much
like everything else is in Underland, and no one has any idea whether
they all lead to the same place.

"IT'S ONLY A DREAM."

WHITE RABBIT

THE WHITE RABBIT, McTwisp, is forever hopping hither and thither – after all, there are Alices to find and trumpets to blow. Stylish, squeamish and ever-punctual, court page McTwisp never leaves home without his pocket watch... and a suitably dapper outfit.

Well-groomed ear

Lucky rabbit paw

On the Hop

The White Rabbit can always be relied upon to do a job properly. He is chosen to go up into the real world and find the "real" Alice. It is no easy task – McTwisp almost gets eaten by other animals, and the least he expects is some gratitude!

"I TOLD YOU SHE'S THE RIGHT ALICE."

22

The Rabbit Hole

McTwisp has been searching high and low for the right Alice so he can lead her to the rabbit hole and down into Underland. Luckily for McTwisp, once he has found Alice, it doesn't take long for her curiosity to get the better of her. She runs after the White Rabbit, peers into the hole, and is promptly pulled into it!

Alice's journey down the rabbit hole is a hair-raising one! The rabbit hole is full of the strange things that McTwisp hoards there, including cracked mirrors, demonic masks and a monkey's hand.

As well as his watch, the White Rabbit also carries a trumpet. He sounds it to announce arrivals at state events or even to declare the start of a battle, though fretful McTwisp isn't particularly fond of these occasions.

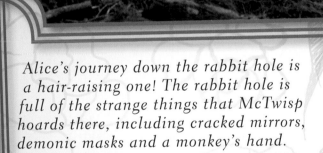

Gold-plated finish

Court Page

Quick, efficient and organised, McTwisp makes an excellent court page. He served in the White Queen's court as her personal page and enjoyed the level of responsibility – and the pristine uniform.

WONDERFUL UNDERLAND
Taking her first steps into Underland, Alice finds herself surrounded by massive mushrooms and giant Talking Flowers that have human faces. It is a strange and beautiful land – and only the beginning of Alice's wonderful adventure.

"LITTLE IMPOSTER!
PRETENDING TO BE ALICE!"

DORMOUSE

MALLYMKUN MAY BE a dormouse but she is certainly not mousy! This feisty creature is determined, brave and always *en garde*. When she is not taking tea with the Mad Hatter and the March Hare, she is busy sharpening her hatpin, donning her breeches and preparing for the next battle.

Daring Dormouse
Mallymkun is brave and defiant. Whether it is fighting a beast like the Bandersnatch or contemplating how to escape her imprisonment by the Red Queen's Knave, the Dormouse refuses to give in. Utterly fearless, Mallymkun will never beg for mercy.

"I DON'T TAKE ORDERS...."

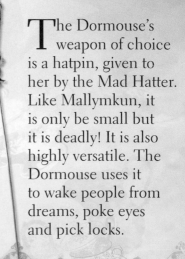

Partners in Crime
Mallymkun is the Mad Hatter's sidekick. She brings him back to reality when he gets crazy. The Hatter considers Mallymkun to be just a close friend, but she is secretly in love with the Hatter.

The Dormouse's weapon of choice is a hatpin, given to her by the Mad Hatter. Like Mallymkun, it is only be small but it is deadly! It is also highly versatile. The Dormouse uses it to wake people from dreams, poke eyes and pick locks.

This sharp hatpin could take someone's eye out – and it has!

The Bandersnatch's eye is kept tied to Mallymkun's belt.

Bull's-eye

There is nothing meek about this mouse! The Dormouse's battle with the Red Queen's beast, the Bandersnatch, is her greatest to date. As soon as she saw Alice in trouble, she pounced on the Bandersnatch and stabbed him in the eye with her hatpin. Now Mallymkun wears the eye as a trophy – and a warning to others who dare to cross her path.

The Red Queen's colors are worn reluctantly.

The Bandersnatch meets its match in the Dormouse. What Mallymkun lacks in size, she more than makes up for with sharp sword skills.

TWEEDLEDUM AND TWEEDLEDEE

IT IS VIRTUALLY impossible to tell Tweedledum and Tweedledee apart. However, this contrary pair might look alike and speak alike but that doesn't mean that they think alike – if Dum says "east to Queast" you can be sure that Dee will say "south to Snud".

Caught in the Middle
The bickering Tweedledum and Tweedledee both want to escort Alice to the Caterpillar, Absolem – it's simply not fair if one gets to do it and the other does not. According to the White Rabbit, their contrariness is a family trait, but the Tweedles are sure to disagree with him on this point!

Extra large trousers for extra large waist

"CONTRARIWISE, I BELIEVE IT SO…"

Snatched!

Tweedledum and Tweedledee are snatched by the Red Queen's screeching Jubjub bird, part monkey-eating eagle and part ostrich, and taken to the Red Queen's castle in Salazen Grum. If they thought the Jubjub bird was scary, wait until they meet the Red Queen!

Team Tweedle

When they are not talking in opposites Dee and Dum are pinching and poking each other. In fact, the only time these two aren't bickering is when they are called into battle. They make a surprisingly good team and fight in perfect unison.

Fatboys

The Red Queen thinks that Tweedledee and Tweedledum, or her "Fatboys", are hilarious. She paints red faces and orders them to speak. Still, it could be worse – she could have ordered their heads to be chopped off!

Black-and-white stripes are one thing the Tweedles do agree on.

29

CATERPILLAR

ABSOLEM IS THE WISEST being in Underland. Everyone trusts this blue caterpillar and they turn to him for his insightful advice. So, who better to be the keeper of the legendary Oraculum? He is also the perfect one to explain to Alice her destiny: she is the person who must kill the evil Jabberwocky with the Vorpal Sword, as written in the Oraculum.

Big Thinker

Most individuals who meet the Caterpillar think he is very serious, but he has been known to collapse in heaps of giggles when tickled. At other times, this caterpillar can be found contemplating his own mortality. Absolem knows that he is coming to the end of this life, but that a new life awaits him as a beautiful blue butterfly.

Mushrooms come in many different colours and sizes.

Perfect Perch

Any philosopher needs a restful place to contemplate. Absolem can usually be found sitting atop a mushroom, be it one in the Mushroom Forest or the White Queen's topiary mushroom.

"NOTHING WAS EVER ACCOMPLISHED WITH TEARS."

The Oraculum

The Oraculum is an ancient parchment that tells about every day since the beginning of time. This astonishing document shows what has happened, what will happen and what is currently happening. Absolem guards the parchment with great care.

ORACULUM

IMAGINE A COMPENDIUM that could reveal the past, present and future of Underland. The Oraculum does exactly that. This ancient parchment scroll chronicles the major events of each and every day since the Beginning. Each event is depicted by a beautiful illustration.

The fearsome Jabberwocky before he shoots fire at the Hightopp Clan of Underland on the Horunvendush Day.

Hightopp hat

The March Hare enjoying a soothing cup of tea.

The Hightopp Clan go around the Maypole on Horunvendush Day.

Not-so-ordinary Oraculum

The Oraculum's black-and-white detailed illustrations depict each and every day. At first glance it might look ordinary, but when the Oraculum is opened each illustration comes to life!

Alice's Fate

Alice sees her future right before her very eyes when the Caterpillar shows her the Frabjous Day in the Oraculum. This is the day that Alice will slay the Jabberwocky. The illustration clearly shows a knight with long blonde hair victoriously standing atop a slain Jabberwocky!

"IT LOOKS SO ORDINARY FOR AN ORACLE."

Absolem shows Alice the Griblig Day in the Oraculum. The illustration shows the Tweedles, the March Hare, Alice and the Dodo looking at the Oraculum at the exact same moment!

The Mad Hatter at the Tea Party that has been going on for years.

The Dormouse holding on to her super-sharp hatpin.

BANDERSNATCH

IT IS FAIR TO SAY that the Red Queen has a lot of enemies. That's why she keeps a vicious guard dog. The Bandersnatch is a huge, horrifying creature that strikes terror in all who live in Underland. With its thunderous roar and razor-sharp teeth, it is a terrifying sight to behold except to a tiny Dormouse....

Big Barrier
Everything about the Bandersnatch is big and strong! The Bandersnatch's smell is so potent, it is enough to knock out anyone within breathing distance, while its huge roar can scare a person witless. If Alice survives all that, there is always the danger that the Bandersnatch might eat her for breakfast!

Mesh net keeps the eyeball secure.

Alice needs the Vorpal Sword in order to slay the Jabberwocky. Unfortunately, the key to the box that houses the sword hangs around the Bandersnatch's neck!

When the Bandersnatch tries to attack Alice, the Dormouse bravely rescues her by stabbing the beast in the eye with her hatpin. As the Dormouse pulls the hatpin out, the Bandersnatch's whole eye pops out, too! She is so pleased that she wears it as a souvenir on her breeches.

On Guard

The Bandersnatch prevents trespassers from entering the Red Queen's castle. It might be furry, but it is definitely not cuddly – one look at this ugly beast is usually enough to scare off any unwanted visitors.

Shark-like teeth stained with blood

Big Softy

Despite the Dormouse's attempts to save Alice, the Bandersnatch lashes out at Alice with its razor-sharp claws. Amazingly, when Alice later returns the eyeball to the Bandersnatch, it changes from vicious beast to gentle giant and licks her wound clean. Maybe its bark is worse than its bite!

JABBERWOCKY

THIS TERRIFYING CREATURE is the Red Queen's darling pet and her ultimate weapon. She has used the brutal Jabberwocky to destroy the Mad Hatter's family – the Hightopp Clan – and the people of Underland live in fear of this vicious creature. The Jabberwocky can only be slain with the Vorpal Sword, but few dare to get near this fanged, fearsome being.

The Vorpal Sword is locked in an ornately engraved box and is guarded by the Bandersnatch.

Frabjous Day

Alice doesn't believe the Caterpillar when he shows her the Oraculum and says that she is the one who will kill the Jabberwocky with the Vorpal Sword on the Frabjous Day. When the Mad Hatter also tells Alice a tale from the Outlands that describes her defeat of the beast, she begins to worry.

Ancient Enemy

The Vorpal Sword is the only weapon that can kill the Jabberwocky and it must be wielded by the correct individual. The sword is beautifully crafted: its hilt is adorned with blue jewels and its blade is studded with pale stones. The sword is exceedingly sharp, but cannot be used for any purpose other than to slay the Jabberwocky.

Fearsome Beast

The Red Queen's "Jabberbabywocky" is nowhere near as helpless as a baby. One whip of the Jabberwocky's sharply pronged tail can fell a bystander, while its ability to shoot fire leaves its foes burned to a crisp. The brutal beast swoops down on its prey, with its eyes aflame and its long sharp claws at the ready.

The Jabberwocky is not simply a senseless slayer. Surprisingly, this frightening beast can speak, and very eloquently at that. Alice is shocked, though she should be used to talking creatures by now – Underland is full of them!

"So my OLD FOE, we meet on the BATTLEFIELD once again."

CREEPY CROSSROADS

The gardens of Underland are a world away from the beautifully manicured
grounds of Lord and Lady Ascot's estate. Underland is wild, overgrown,
slightly eerie – and so much more exciting than the perfectly neat and terribly
proper gardens of London.

"EAST TO QUEAST... SOUTH TO SNUD."

RED QUEEN

IRACEBETH, THE RED QUEEN OF CRIMS, wasn't always heartless. Her sister, the White Queen, remembers a time when she even got along with 'Racie, but things are different now. The Red Queen's study of Dominion Over Living Things has made her a feared leader, and her frequent cry of "Off with his head!" means her scared subjects obey her every command.

Bighead
The most striking thing about the Red Queen is the size of her head – it is huge! Alice thinks it is bloated and the White Queen thinks it is a growth, but neither would say so to Iracebeth. The Red Queen is so obsessed that she has a mirror that makes her humongous head look smaller and a room of hats to cover her gigantic globe!

Heart to Heart
The Red Queen only has eyes for the Knave of Hearts. The feeling is not mutual, but the Red Queen knows they will be together one day.

The Red Queen rules from her ornate throne, attended by frog footmen and a fish butler.

"IT IS FAR BETTER TO BE FEARED THAN LOVED."

Tiny crown perches on top of the Red Queen's huge head.

For the Chop

Whether it is catching a frog footman stealing her squimberry tarts or seeing someone flirting with the Knave, the Red Queen's response is always the same – off with their heads! This ruthless ruler is fixated with heads!

Ornamental sceptre

Iracebeth rarely sees things favourably, even through these rose-coloured spectacles. Mostly she sees red.

Red Rule

The Red Queen is not a popular monarch. She removed her sister from the throne and unleashed the Jabberwocky on the Hightopp Clan, leaving the Mad Hatter as the only survivor. The Underland Underground Resistance exists to overthrow Iracebeth: Downal wyth Bluddy Behg Hid!

RED QUEEN'S COURT

To become a courtier to the Red Queen only one crucial criteria has to be met – no inflated egos, just inflated body parts. However, there is only room for one big head at court and that is the Red Queen's! Life at court is very competitive and extremely tiring. It is the courtier's job to praise and flatter the Red Queen at all times because there is always a danger that she may utter those infamous words of hers at any moment....

Court Rules
All of the Red Queen's courtiers are required to have extra-large features. It is also a rule that their faces are painted and powdered, so that they are in keeping with the Red Queen's preferred style.

Lady Long Ears
Lady Long Ears is the Red Queen's eyes and (big) ears around court. She soon has a long face when large Alice arrives and the Red Queen declares that she is her new favourite. So when Lady Long Ears finds out that the Knave of Hearts has a soft spot for Alice, she makes sure that the Red Queen knows all about it.

Red Knights
The Red Queen has many enemies. Her knights in red armour are always standing guard around court, ready to take orders and defend their queen.

The Red Knights are never without their sharp spears. They use them against any intruders who enter the Red Queen's court unannounced. Don't be fooled by the heart-shaped tips – these spears are definitely not used with love.

Knave of Hearts

The Red Queen wants to be feared by all who know her, except one – her Knave, Ilosovic Stayne. Unfortunately for the Red Queen, Stayne is not in love with her. In fact, she makes him shudder. He would much rather die than spend the rest of his life with her. Stayne is tasked with finding Alice and bringing her to the Red Queen, unharmed. Iracebeth wants to have the pleasure of beheading Alice herself.

The violent Knave of Hearts is not one to choose his battles carefully. Any opportunity to unsheathe his sword is seized upon by the Knave with relish. However, he likes his victims to put up a bit of a fight. Where's the fun in battle if there is no weeping or begging? Those are the best bits!

This portly courtier is very proud of his protruding belly. However, it is actually fake and is held in place by straps. He would much rather carry extra weight around his middle to please the Red Queen than lose the weight of his head.

45

RED QUEEN'S CASTLE

SITTING ON THE TEMPESTUOUS shore of the Crimson Sea in Salazen Grum is a dark and menacing sight. Welcome to the Red Queen's castle, where the Red Queen rules over her kingdom. Enter at your peril, for it is not a place for the fainthearted. You have been warned....

Grizzly Welcome

There's only one way to get to the castle doors and that is across a grim moat, which is filled with a red liquid that looks strangely like blood. Stepping stones in the form of heads of the Red Queen's unlucky visitors are kindly provided to get across. The Red Queen certainly doesn't make it easy for her guests!

The Red Queen's crest displayed on the flags is a heart in flames.

High walls to keep intruders out

The Throne Room is where the Red Queen makes all her important decisions, which more often than not involve the words "head" and "off with!"

Grim moat is definitely not for swimming in!

"I AM NOT A PATIENT MONARCH!"

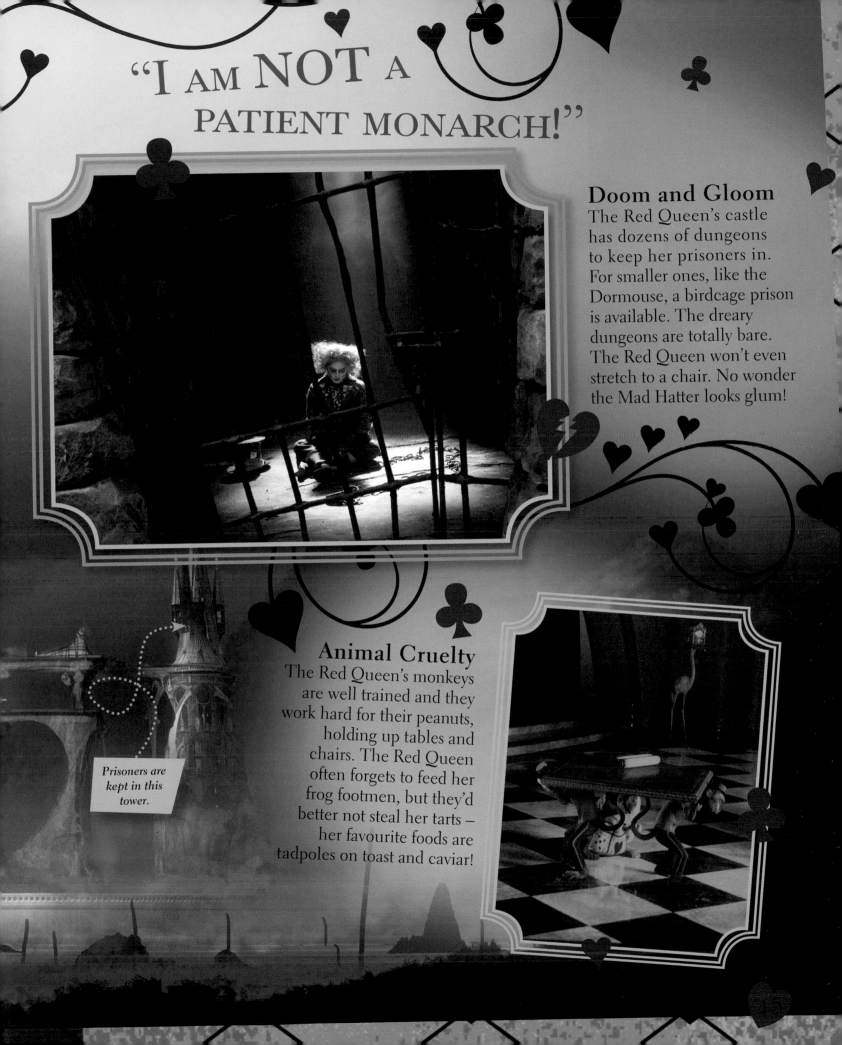

Doom and Gloom

The Red Queen's castle has dozens of dungeons to keep her prisoners in. For smaller ones, like the Dormouse, a birdcage prison is available. The dreary dungeons are totally bare. The Red Queen won't even stretch to a chair. No wonder the Mad Hatter looks glum!

Prisoners are kept in this tower.

Animal Cruelty

The Red Queen's monkeys are well trained and they work hard for their peanuts, holding up tables and chairs. The Red Queen often forgets to feed her frog footmen, but they'd better not steal her tarts – her favourite foods are tadpoles on toast and caviar!

COURTLY CROQUET

ORDERING HEADS TO be chopped off every minute of every day can be exhausting! So the Red Queen likes nothing more than taking some time out from her busy schedule to partake in a leisurely game of croquet.

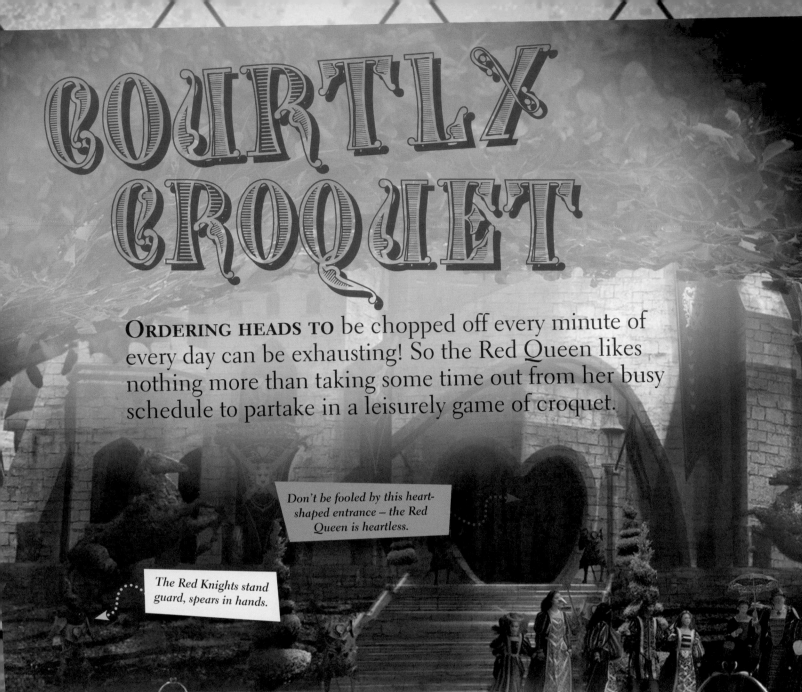

Don't be fooled by this heart-shaped entrance – the Red Queen is heartless.

The Red Knights stand guard, spears in hands.

Flamingos hold up the arches.

Cruel Contest

The Red Queen's croquet game is very different from the traditional game. Look closely at this sad sight – miserable flamingos are used as mallets and unfortunate hedgehogs are tied into balls. The Red Queen is much amused!

The Red Queen's odd-looking
minions look on.

Staff watch on
as the Red Queen
shows off.

Flamingo is used
as a mallet.

The chance to get some fresh air outside
the dark and dingy castle is a relief to
the Red Queen's court. The Red Queen
is no croquet champion however, and she
completely misses the hoop! But her staff
like their heads attached to their necks so
they keep quiet. They won't get the chance
to swing a mallet because she is not a team
player. Only queens are allowed to play
– that way, there can be only one winner!

MAD HATTER

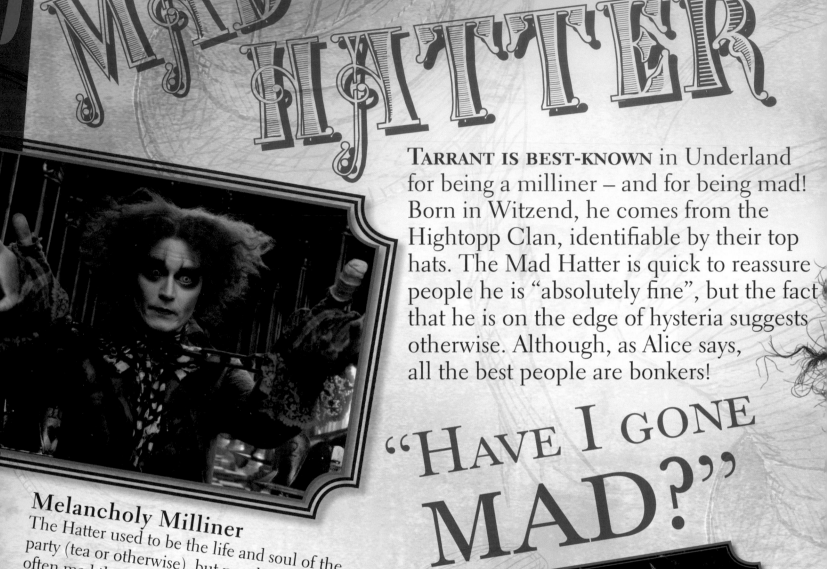

TARRANT IS BEST-KNOWN in Underland for being a milliner – and for being mad! Born in Witzend, he comes from the Hightopp Clan, identifiable by their top hats. The Mad Hatter is quick to reassure people he is "absolutely fine", but the fact that he is on the edge of hysteria suggests otherwise. Although, as Alice says, all the best people are bonkers!

"HAVE I GONE MAD?"

Melancholy Milliner
The Hatter used to be the life and soul of the party (tea or otherwise), but now he is more often mad than happy. However, the Hatter has promised that when the White Queen rules once more, he will Futterwacken like never before.

Suffering Soul
Tarrant's descent into madness can be traced back to the Horunvendush Day when the Red Queen set her Jabberwocky on the Hightopp Clan. The Hatter was the only survivor and his feelings of guilt and rage drove him over the edge.

Friends Indeed
The Mad Hatter is the only one who believes that Alice is the Alice who visited Underland before. The pair care for each other, but they will never be compatible – Alice is always too tall or too small!

Tarrant's top hat has plenty of hatpins stuck in it.

Heads Up!

The Dormouse has kept the Hatter calm when he has lost his head, and he wants to return the favour – before she loses hers. Tarrant nobly defends Mallymkun when the Red Queen picks the pair out for execution.

The Hatter's bright green eyes always look slightly crazed.

Top Hatter

Whether it is a bonnet, a cloche or a boater you are after, the Mad Hatter is head and shoulders above the rest. Tarrant feels best when he is hatting. He has worked for both the White Queen and the Red Queen and on heads large and small.

49

A Dream Come True

All the dreams that Alice had of talking dodos and grinning cats were never as vivid as this one. Strange landscapes, fantastical castles and bizarre creatures were to be expected; the chance to make friends that she will never forget was not.

"I'LL MISS YOU WHEN I WAKE UP."

COURT HATTER

EVERY COURT NEEDS a hatter and when it comes to making hats, the Mad Hatter is the best in all of Underland. No head is too big or too small for his marvellous millinery. There is no doubt that his creations are fit for a queen!

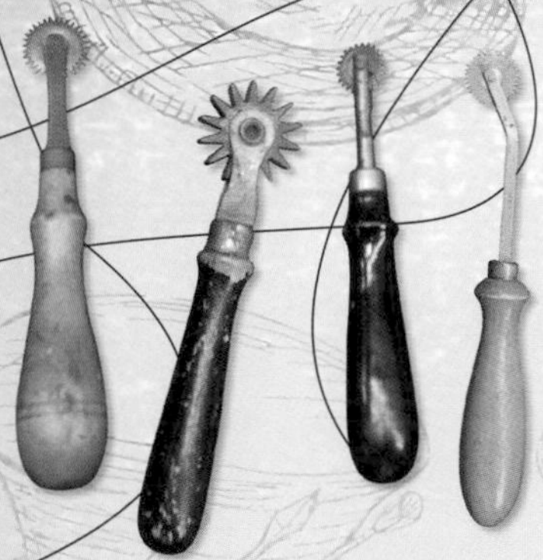

Special millinery tools are used to make pretty silk flowers to adorn the hats.

Fancy hatpin

Sad Hat

The Mad Hatter's family, the Hightopp Clan, had always been employed at court, but all that remains of his clan now is this burned and trampled top hat. Without this hat on his head, the Mad Hatter feels completely and utterly lost.

Hatter's Hightopp Clan number

Bright silk material adds colour and hides some of the burns.

Hatter Originals

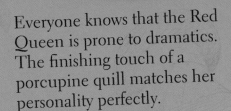

With his hat stretcher in hand, the Hatter gets hatting and sets about making fabulous and fantastic creations for the Red Queen's humongous head.

Everyone knows that the Red Queen is prone to dramatics. The finishing touch of a porcupine quill matches her personality perfectly.

The Hatter is nothing if not visionary. He knows that leaves are not just for trees – they make fabulous decorations too!

The Hatter knows what suits his clients best and he has noticed the Red Queen's penchant for the colour red.

Black and white has always been a classic combination. The Hatter adds some pink netting to this hat to please the Red Queen. Well, pink is almost red!

"THE ABSOLUTE BEST WAY TO TRAVEL IS BY HAT."

It takes more than skill and talent to construct a hat, and no hatter would be without all the tools of the trade. The Hatter keeps his trusty chalk, thimble and needles in beautifully decorated, ornate cases. To cut some of the finest silks in the world a blunt pair of scissors just will not do – they must be super-sharp. But it's best not to upset the Hatter when he has these to hand. He has been known to cut all his hard work to shreds in a mad frenzy!

Pot contains silver thimble, needles and small scissors.

Silver case is engraved with flowers.

Hefty dressmaking scissors

CHESHIRE CAT

THE CHESHIRE CAT doesn't need nine lives – he is perfectly happy with the one he's got! Serene Chessur can often be found lounging around and grinning away. That is if you can see him, as Chess can make himself disappear at will. Unlike his friends, Chessur is not part of the Underland Underground Resistance; this laid-back feline prefers not to get involved in politics.

Now You See Him
Chessur is the cat's pyjamas. He can appear as a disembodied head or as a complete cat. He can even disappear entirely. This remarkable talent certainly comes in useful when he has to make a quick getaway.

The Cat and the Hat

The Mad Hatter and the Cheshire Cat have a tricky relationship. When the Hightopp Clan was killed by the Jabberwocky, Chessur disappeared from the scene, fearing for his life. The Hatter blames Chess for what happened that day, but Chess hopes to win back the Hatter's trust.

Chessur's mesmerising eyes are the last thing to disappear.

Broad Cheshire Cat grin

Suave Feline

The Cheshire Cat is a dapper tabby. He is eloquently spoken, always smiles and is gentlemanly to Alice. When Alice is injured by the Bandersnatch, Chessur is there to tie her bloody wound with his handkerchief. He even keeps the cat in the bag about his loathing of blood to help his new pal.

"ALL THIS TALK OF BLOOD AND SLAYING HAS PUT ME OFF MY TEA."

Courage of a Lion

Chessur has learned his lesson. He wants to show that he can be brave and offers to be the one to slay the Jabberwocky. This fearless feline also takes the place of the Hatter when he is headed for the guillotine – after all, you can't chop off a head that has no body!

MARCH HARE

THACKERY, THE MARCH HARE, is a jumpy creature who spends a lot of his time scared! Born in Witzend, the March Hare was a member of the White Queen's court. Now he is the host of Underland's longest Tea Party, which has been going on for years. Even so, people still arrive late for tea, which does little for Thackery's anxiety issues.

Home Sweet Home
It is easy to spot Thackery's house – it looks just like him. The house is thatched with fur, the front looks like a hare's face (with windows like eyes) and the windmill sails resemble large ears! Like the March Hare, the house is wary of new people and has been known to tap Thackery on the head when a stranger comes to visit.

Head Chef
Thackery is an excellent chef. Afternoon (or all-day) tea is his speciality, but he also makes tasty soup.

"YOU'RE ALL LATE FOR TEA!"

The March Hare's Tea Party is the longest in Underland history. The tablecloths are threadbare, the ceramic plates and teapots are chipped with age and the guest list has barely changed. If Thackery had known the party would last this long, he would never have started it!

Large ears twitch anxiously.

Mad as a March Hare

The March Hare is happiest sipping a cup of sweet tea and he hates anything that may spoil this enjoyment. When he has been slaving over a hot stove, the least he expects is for his guests to be on time. If they are not, they had better watch out for flying teapots and pepper mills – the March Hare goes hopping mad with latecomers!

Thackery always has a cup of tea in his paw.

Overused, broken plate

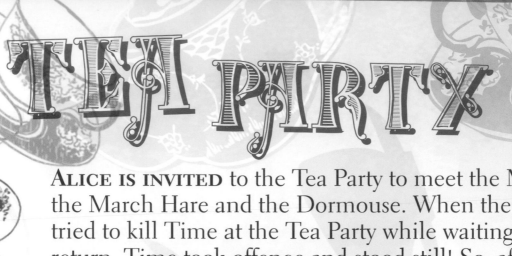

TEA PARTY

ALICE IS INVITED to the Tea Party to meet the Mad Hatter, the March Hare and the Dormouse. When the Mad Hatter tried to kill Time at the Tea Party while waiting for Alice's return, Time took offence and stood still! So, after years of waiting, the gathering has lost its party atmosphere, but the return of Alice soon stirs things up.

Tea Time

The table napkins may be stained and the crockery chipped, but there is still lots of wonderful food on offer at the Tea Party. Sandwiches, cakes, biscuits, raspberry jam and – of course – plenty of tea are sure to keep even the fussiest of guests happy!

Tea is known for its soothing and calming qualities, but years of drinking the stuff doesn't seem to have done much for the March Hare's nerves!

Handpainted decoration

Tiny Alice

The Knave of Hearts gate crashes the Tea Party, looking for Alice. The Mad Hatter quickly forces Alice to drink the shrinking juice Pishalver and stuffs her into a teapot. The Knave would never think to look there!

"YOU'RE ABSOLUTELY ALICE! I'D KNOW YOU ANYWHERE."

Mad Trio

While Alice is hiding in the teapot, the Mad Hatter, the Dormouse and the March Hare attempt to put the Knave of Hearts off her scent by singing silly songs. This seems to confirm to the Knave that they are all mad!

The saucer is enormous compared to Alice when she is just six inches high.

WHITE QUEEN

Just one look from Mirana's pretty eyes is all it takes for her to get what she wants. Even the Red Queen's unusual furniture isn't safe from her powerful beauty!

MIRANA, THE WHITE QUEEN, is everything that her sister, the Red Queen, is not – beautiful, gentle and kind. Mirana is adored by the people of Underland. They are willing to risk their lives in order for her to rule again.

Rivals

Alice has always got along with her sister, Margaret; Mirana has not been so lucky. The White Queen's beauty turns her sister green with envy. Mirana just wants her crown back. All she needs is a champion to step forth and slay the Jabberwocky. If only she could find one….

Mirana is not just a pretty face. Her mother taught her how to concoct medicinal cures and transformational potions. She prepares Pishalver, a shrinking juice, for Alice by mixing together gruesome things, including buttered fingers, a pinch of worm fat and White Queen's spit.

Despite having a jar full of spare eyeballs, Mirana still needs her spyglass to keep a lookout on all the comings and goings at her castle.

Loyal Friend
Bayard the bloodhound is forever faithful to the White Queen and her cause, even when he is otherwise tied up. His family is behind bars at the Red Queen's castle – if he brings Alice to the Red Queen, he will earn their freedom. But like the loyal friend he is, he leads Alice to the White Queen, Vorpal Sword in her hand.

Shiny white curls

Mouse is considered a friend.

"WE DON'T HAVE TO FIGHT."

Healing Power

Mirana's power is in the healing arts and it would go against her vows to bring harm to any living thing. So all creatures great and small would be safe under her rule, with the exception of a few ugly bugs!

WHITE QUEEN'S CASTLE

SITTING HIGH ON a hilltop overlooking the magnificent kingdom of Marmoreal is the White Queen's dazzling castle. A winding path leads up to the imposing castle with its domed turrets and stained glass windows, which let in lots of light. It is warm and welcoming – much like the White Queen herself.

Checkmate

The White Queen's castle is made entirely out of white marble. The White Queen has chosen a "chess" theme – giant chess pieces sit atop huge boulders, and even the lawn is mown to look just like a chessboard.

The long drive allows visitors to marvel at the stunning castle.

On the Boil

Mirana has a huge kitchen where she concocts her potions. The March Hare is Mirana's cook so, unless guests want to wear their supper, they should arrive on time!

"WELCOME TO MARMOREAL."

With its many turrets and spires, the White Queen's castle looks imposing, but there are many wonderful things to see. A keen animal lover, Mirana has a topiary garden filled with trees and shrubs shaped into animals, including a giraffe and a flamingo. If her trees ever look sad, she has her staff talk to them in a kindly manner to cheer them up. In the Throne Room is the White Knight's armour. It has been here since Shatterky, the day the White Queen was banished to Marmoreal. It just needs the Vorpal Sword to be brought home to complete it.

Chess pieces are carved into the castle.

Serene lake of fresh water – there's no danger of finding chopped off heads here.

Pristine chequered lawn

UNDERLAND

WHEN ALICE FIRST STEPPED through that small door she entered a land where time can stand still, animals can talk, and adventures are always waiting to happen. Underland is unique – no wonder Alice thinks she is dreaming.

The Round Hall

Alice's journey into Underland has a bizarre beginning. After falling into the Round Hall, Alice sees lots of ornate locked doors and one little door behind a curtain, but there is only one key.

Talking Flowers

It is not only the creatures that can talk in Underland. The flowers have human faces and like nothing more than a good gossip. The Talking Flowers grow in a garden that is home to a green pig and enormous gnats.

The Tulgey Wood

The Tulgey Wood is a dark and barren place. Visiting the Tulgey Wood always brings back sad memories for the Mad Hatter. It was here that his clan perished on Horunvendush Day.

Strange Beauty

Underland might look beautiful, but sometimes even beauty has a dark side. The White Queen's garden, with its topiary animals, is probably one of the safest spots to be in.

The Mushroom Forest

There are many different forests in Underland. Perhaps the strangest is the Mushroom Forest, where the mushrooms grow as tall as the trees. Absolem the Caterpillar can often be found sitting atop one of the mushrooms here.

O FRABIOUS DAY

THE RED QUEEN'S SUBJECTS have been waiting a long time for Alice to return to Underland and for the Frabjous Day to dawn – the day when Alice will slay the Jabberwocky. Then the White Queen will rule again and everyone will Futterwacken! The Mad Hatter is the only one who believes that this Alice is the true Alice. Now it is up to Alice to prove him right.

Large silver shield belongs to the White Knight.

Alice Awakes

Even though it is written in the Oraculum that Alice must slay the Jabberwocky, the White Queen tells Alice that the choice is hers. Alice finds it all a bit overwhelming and seeks advice from Absolem. She begins to remember that her dream of Wonderland, as she called it, was not a dream – she has been here before. She is Alice At Last!

The Vorpal Sword has a mind of its own. All Alice has to do is hold on tight!

Battle Ruins

The battle ruins in the Tulgey Wood are the perfect place for a combat of epic proportions. They are brimming with the history of all the previous battles of Underland. The ancient remains afford ample opportunities for Alice to conceal herself from the fearsome Jabberwocky.

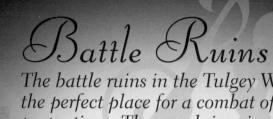

The White Queen doesn't want to battle with her sister, but Iracebeth has other ideas. Like a spoilt child, the Red Queen won't surrender her crown without a fight.

Let Battle Commence

Alice cannot believe that she will be able to slay the Jabberwocky. While the pair fight, Alice remembers other things in Underland that she would have thought were impossible. With a newfound confidence, Alice cuts off the Jabberwocky's head using the Vorpal Sword. The reign of Bluddy Behg Hid is finally at an end and the White Queen banishes her sister and the Knave to the Outlands forever. Callou, callay!

NEW ADVENTURES

ALICE HAS HAD the most amazing adventure in Underland but she must say goodbye to her new companions and return to the real world. After all, there are important things she must tell her family and friends. Alice's adventure has boosted her confidence and courage. She is now ready to take on the world and stand up for what she wants.

Real World

Alice chooses to drink a drop of the Jabberwocky's blood, which allows her to return home. She wakes up back in the real world, dangling from a rabbit hole. Her dress is torn and filthy and her hair is dishevelled, which confuses Alice. What could she have been doing? She thinks she may have fallen and bumped her head. All memory of her adventure in Underland has completely vanished.

Alice Returns
When Alice returns to the party, the guests are shocked by her appearance. But Alice doesn't care what she looks like or about her improper behaviour. She even dances a Futterwacken in front of the guests!

Ambitious Alice

Alice has a proposal for Lord Ascot. She thinks that his company should be the first to trade with China. Lord Ascot sees that Alice has inherited her father's vision and ambition. He is so impressed with Alice's confidence, he offers her an apprenticeship with the company. Her father would have been proud.

Alice is now an assured young woman who knows exactly what she believes in. She tells Hamish that she cannot marry him, lets Lady Ascot know that, unlike her, she *loves* rabbits and makes sure Lowell realises she will be watching him very closely. While dispensing her frank words, Alice can't help noticing the Chattaways' resemblance to some funny boys she met in a dream....

"I'LL FIND SOMETHING USEFUL TO DO WITH MY LIFE."

New Horizons

Alice has said goodbye to her friends and family and is ready to set sail into her future with Lord Ascot's company in China. Before she leaves, a beautiful blue butterfly lands on her shoulder. Alice recognises Absolem in his new form, come to say goodbye. Maybe Alice hasn't forgotten her new friends after all.

Alice's mother and sister, and also Lord Ascot, gather to bid farewell to Alice as she embarks on her new adventure.

ALICE

THROUGH

THE

LOOKING

GLASS

THROUGH THE LOOKING GLASS

ALICE'S ADVENTURES IN Underland brought out her bravery and independence. She returned more confident and empowered than before, and set out to carve herself a place in the world, unrestrained by the social expectations she is expected to follow.

She has excelled as a sea captain and businesswoman, exploring the East and surviving by her wits. But Alice arrives home to discover that change isn't quite as easy as she thought. Her family faces financial trouble and her new-found freedoms are under threat.

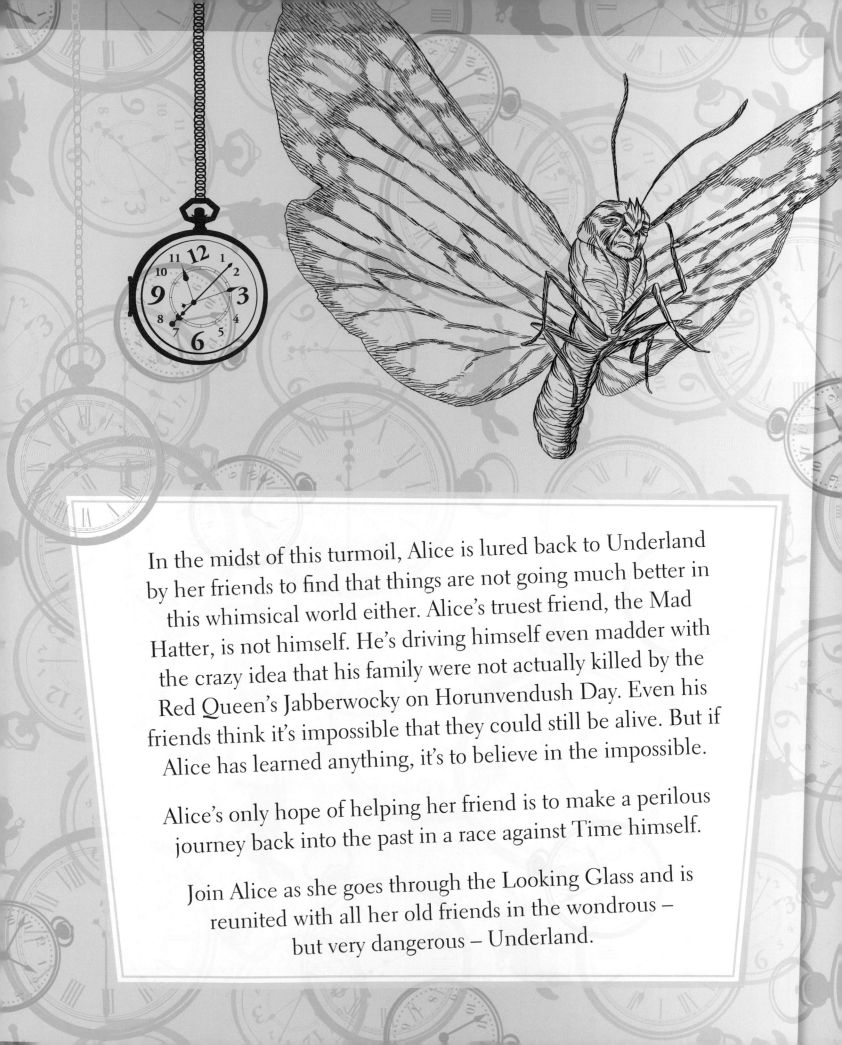

In the midst of this turmoil, Alice is lured back to Underland by her friends to find that things are not going much better in this whimsical world either. Alice's truest friend, the Mad Hatter, is not himself. He's driving himself even madder with the crazy idea that his family were not actually killed by the Red Queen's Jabberwocky on Horunvendush Day. Even his friends think it's impossible that they could still be alive. But if Alice has learned anything, it's to believe in the impossible.

Alice's only hope of helping her friend is to make a perilous journey back into the past in a race against Time himself.

Join Alice as she goes through the Looking Glass and is reunited with all her old friends in the wondrous – but very dangerous – Underland.

ALICE THE SEA CAPTAIN

IT IS THE AGE of sea travel. Foreign lands offer exotic goods for trading and there are fortunes to be made! Young Alice Kingsleigh has her father's entrepreneurial vision and ambition. She has spent three years at sea developing trade routes in the East for her benefactor, Lord Ascot. Now she is back, with big plans for business expansion.

Sturdy Clipper
This fast-sailing clipper belonged to Alice's father and is her ticket to freedom and adventure. Out on the ocean, no one thinks sea captain is an unsuitable occupation for a lady – especially for such a natural mariner as Alice.

Helen Kingsleigh
Alice is happy to be reunited with her mother, but they still disagree about her future. Helen believes the only way for a woman to have a good life – and a secure financial future – is to marry well.

Kindly Lord Ascot has died, leaving his mean, pompous son in charge. Hamish has no interest in Alice's ideas – particularly since she rejected his marriage proposal.

Intrepid Explorer

Fiercely confident Alice was just the person to forge the future of Lord Ascot's business. Her belief that nothing is impossible spurred her to see new opportunities. As a capable sea captain, she thought nothing of braving hazardous storms, navigating perilous waters or dodging pirates. Alice led her crew through danger time and time again.

Charles Kingsleigh's atlas reveals so many exciting places to explore. Enterprising Alice can see untapped potential for more trading routes along the Wu river and in Malay.

Guard protects hand.

"THE WORLD HAS OPENED TO US, BUT WE MUST MOVE QUICKLY!"

Life at sea is not always plain sailing. Alice carries this sea captain's sword as protection from pirates – and worse!

Charles Kingsleigh's pocket watch is Alice's constant companion and reminder of him. Whenever Alice is afraid, she thinks of her father and his memory gives her the strength to be brave.

Hands stopped moving when Charles died.

ALICE'S PAINTINGS

PAINTING IS A very suitable pastime for a respectable young lady, but Alice's mother, Helen, despairs at her daughter's curious imagination. Why can't she stick to drawing landscapes or bowls of fruit? Little does Helen realise: these are not scenes from Alice's imagination, but memories of her very real visit to Underland.

Alice paints the spot where her adventures in Underland all began… the rabbit hole on the Ascots' grounds, and the white rabbit in a waistcoat that she followed to find it.

Alice doesn't know how to contact her friends like Mallymkun. Painting their portraits helps her to remember them.

Using paint, Alice recreates the sense of being tiny, surrounded by enormous people, gigantic birds and towering mushrooms.

Fleeting glimpses of shapes and colours combine on paper at Alice's hand. Paintings like this one of Tweedledum and Tweedledee help to keep her memories of Underland alive.

This simple watercolour evokes the frightfulness of the Jabberwocky – before Alice's great victory over the beast.

Of everyone in Underland, Alice misses the Hatter the most. She doubts she'll ever meet such a kindred spirit again.

Again, the tubby twins, the rabbit in the blue coat and the curious railings. The same outlandish images keep repeating in Alice's art.

77

WHEN TWO WORLDS COLLIDE

Chinese-style wide, ornate collar

ALICE OFTEN FINDS herself at odds with the world around her. She's too headstrong to blend into English society and is sometimes out of step with the curious ways of Underland, too. She's too independent to worry much about what people think, but it can be tricky juggling two different worlds.

Ascot Mansion

Alice is bursting with fresh business ideas and she can't wait to share them with the influential Ascot family. Although her plans are rejected by stuffy Hamish, his smart house offers a surprise opportunity for Alice: a way back to Underland.

Distinctive Style

Independent Alice likes to express her unique style, no matter who may stare or snigger. For the Ascots' fancy dinner party, she chooses a bright, flamboyant outfit from the East. If it's good enough for a Chinese Empress, then it's good enough for Alice!

Chinese silk embroidered with butterflies and flowers

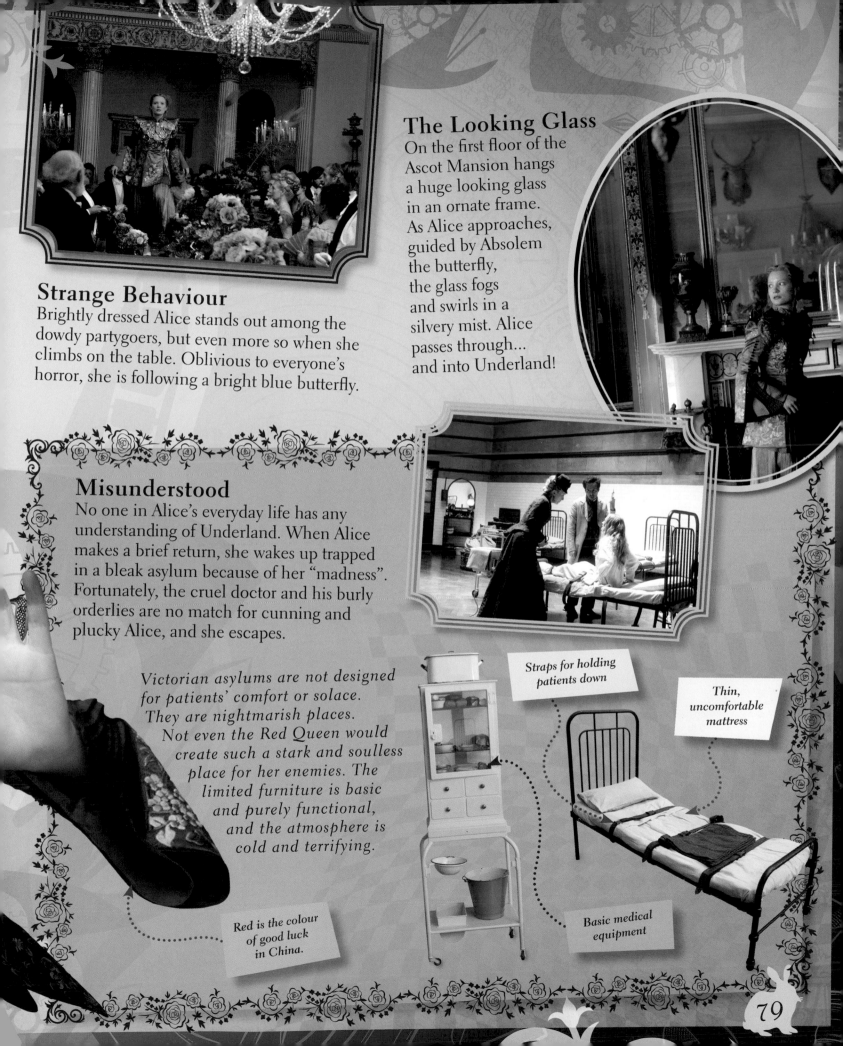

Strange Behaviour

Brightly dressed Alice stands out among the dowdy partygoers, but even more so when she climbs on the table. Oblivious to everyone's horror, she is following a bright blue butterfly.

The Looking Glass

On the first floor of the Ascot Mansion hangs a huge looking glass in an ornate frame. As Alice approaches, guided by Absolem the butterfly, the glass fogs and swirls in a silvery mist. Alice passes through... and into Underland!

Misunderstood

No one in Alice's everyday life has any understanding of Underland. When Alice makes a brief return, she wakes up trapped in a bleak asylum because of her "madness". Fortunately, the cruel doctor and his burly orderlies are no match for cunning and plucky Alice, and she escapes.

Victorian asylums are not designed for patients' comfort or solace. They are nightmarish places. Not even the Red Queen would create such a stark and soulless place for her enemies. The limited furniture is basic and purely functional, and the atmosphere is cold and terrifying.

Red is the colour of good luck in China.

Straps for holding patients down

Thin, uncomfortable mattress

Basic medical equipment

FAMILIAR FACES

ALICE'S OLD FRIENDS are delighted to welcome her back to Underland, but the celebrations don't last long. Something terrible has happened to the Hatter and Alice's friends know that only she can put things right.

The Hatter

The friendly Hatter has always been a lively character, but now he's become quiet and withdrawn. He's lost his muchness: the thing that makes him him. His friends are seriously worried. They can't even raise a smile from him.

Expression shows concern for the Hatter.

Chessur

Alice's pal Chessur is still hanging around, grinning like the cat who got the cream. But even this smiler – known for his toothy grin and whimsical nature – is worried about the Hatter, and hopes Alice can help.

McTwisp

Dapper little McTwisp is hopping with excitement to see his old friend Alice. It could be said that this neat, orderly rabbit is the most rational of the group, but then he does have some truly crazy friends.

As well as beauty, Mirana the White Queen also has the brains to come up with a plan for Alice to help the Hatter. It's so audacious that only she dares suggest it.

"ALICE!
YOU'RE YOU
AND YOU'RE HERE!"

Haughty expression

Absolem's wings enable him to fly to fetch Alice from her world.

Not everyone is so happy to see Alice back. To the Red Queen, Alice is the slayer of her precious Jabberwocky and the reason she is banished from her kingdom. The ruthless Queen wants Alice's head—before she can do any more meddling.

Absolem
Someone has been busy since Alice's last visit. Absolem has transformed from an aging caterpillar to a striking blue butterfly. Now he can look down on everyone from an even higher height. The haughty philosopher still finds Alice a little tiresome, but isn't everyone when you're so wise and important?

81

TARRANT HIGHTOPP

The first hat Tarrant ever made was a tiny creation of blue paper. He gave it to his father as a token of love, but was crushed to believe Zanik threw it away. When he finds it years later in the Tulgey Woods, it becomes a symbol of hope that his family is still alive.

Crumpled blue paper haphazardly glued

Clumsy but whimsical construction

Eager to show anyone how they look in a hat, Tarrant carries this mirror around in his coat pocket.

Zanik's own hat is a sombre affair – hats should be serious, not fun!

SOMETHING IS THE matter with the Hatter. His friends think that grief for his murdered family and guilt from a row with his father have caused him to lose his mind. He has developed the most curious theory: he thinks his family are still alive. What could be madder than that?

"IF THIS HAT SURVIVED, THEN MY FAMILY DID TOO!"

Fussy Father
Zanik Hightopp took his profession as a hatter very seriously. He loved his son, but was often hard on him. His intention was to develop the boy's hatmaking potential, but it led the Hatter to believe he was a disappointment to his father.

The Hightopp Clan

The Hightopp Clan was a proud family of hatmakers —the best in Witzend! Everyone knows the tragic story of how they were slain by the Red Queen's Jabberwocky on Horunvendush Day. Or were they?

Spare hatpins for hatting emergencies

Thimble for sewing

Stain from fabric dye

Heartbroken

Normally such a cheerful, upbeat fellow, the Hatter is fading with heartbreak. He is overjoyed when he sees Alice, though he is still angry and suspicious of everyone else. How can his friends not see his family must still be alive? Surely his Alice will believe him?

TIME

To ALICE'S ASTONISHMENT, Time is a person. He is a tall figure, dressed from top to toe in midnight black. Part-clockwork, he is a mysterious man whose nature is as curious as that of Underland itself. Alice regards Time as a thief, taking her father too early. However, she comes to see that he does give before he takes, and that every day is a gift.

Tall hat adds to Time's stature.

The Chronosphere is Time's responsibility.

Easily Wound Up
Time waits for no man – he's far too impatient. He has no tolerance for anyone who wastes his time and he takes himself far too seriously to have a sense of humour. When Alice's friends tease him, he just gets angry and unleashes his cruel streak.

Time Keeper

Time lives in the Castle of Eternity. Here, he is responsible for keeping the Grand Clock of All Time – and reality – ticking. He is also custodian of the pocket watches that represent each Underlandian. When a person's time is up, Time removes his or her stopped watch from the cacophonous room called "Underlandians: Living" and files it away in the silent chamber "Underlandians: Dead".

Time's Sanctuary
Time's castle is stark and vast, but his sitting room is a cosy haven with oak panels, a roaring fire and overstuffed armchairs. They provide comfort from the dizzying sense of eternity in the void outside.

"I AM TIME! THE INFINITE! THE ETERNAL! THE IMMORTAL!"

Time has a magpie's eye for trinkets. Some he uses to make his sitting room cosy; others he gives as gifts to please his beloved Red Queen.

Cologne for when the Red Queen visits

Jewelled skull of an Underland bird

Pawn chess piece

Knight chess piece

Pink mouthwash

Sceptre gives Time a sense of self-importance.

Decorative silver fretwork

COLOGNE

MOUTHWASH

85

TIME TRAVEL

DEEP WITHIN THE Grand Clock of All Time spins a glowing metallic sphere – the Chronosphere. This magical object powers the clock, but it also holds the secrets of time travel.

Chronosphere

The Chronosphere is the mystical source of order in the Universe. Small enough to fit in your pocket, it can grow into a time machine large enough to carry a person. Alice, a natural sailor, is unfazed by its strange controls. She adjusts the Time Line Panel, grabs the "Pull Me" lever, and blasts away, leaving nothing but a vapour trail.

Sun engraving represents the passing of time.

Design echoes clockwork patterns.

Time Flies

This diagram reveals that time does not just seem to go at different speeds – it actually does. Time is elastic: the older you get, the faster it goes. It also slows down when you are standing in line and really grinds when you're waiting for summer or for a broken heart to heal. And of course, when you are facing a deadline, it zips by in a flash.

Amongst Time's papers are ancient documents and charts that attempt to explain the curious scientific laws of Underland.

Ornately carved throne

Time zones of the Chronosphere

Chronosphere Time Zones

Large, imposing shoulders

Tunnel shows how Underland came to be created out of the Big Bang.

Babbling accounts of how the animals learned to speak and walk like humans

Wise Watchman

Time is appalled at the thought of anyone time traveling: without the Chronosphere to power the Grand Clock, everything could disintegrate into nothingness. Worst of all, if someone's past self sees their future self, then the past, the present and the future will all be history.

Advanced rabbit species is called "bunolgus h. sapien".

TIME TRAVELLER

THE HATTER IS Alice's truest friend and when he's in need, she'll help him no matter what. Alice is so desperate to change the past and help the Hatter's family that she's willing to risk not only herself but the whole fabric of existence too.

New Old Friends
Nothing throws the Hatter. Not even a complete stranger declaring she knows him from when he is older and she is younger. He feels an instant affinity with Alice and welcomes her like the old friend she will be. After all, all the best ones are bonkers.

As the years roll back, so do the ages of Alice's friends. Chessur is now a little fluffy kitten. He has found his paws, but is still working on his vanishing trick.

Father and Son
Alice meets the young Hatter in his father's hat shop. She witnesses his playful frivolity in hatmaking and by contrast, his father's sane, sober, disciplined approach.

88

"I MUST SAVE THE HATTER. WE'RE A 'WE' AND HE NEEDS ME."

Swashbuckler

Stealing Time's Chronosphere and sailing it through the Oceans of Time is just the job for a brave sea captain. However, to Alice's frustration, she discovers Time was right—you cannot change the past, but maybe you can learn from it. If Alice can find out what really happened to the Hightopps, she may be able to work out what can be done to save them.

ROYAL SISTERS

ALL THE PRIVILEGE in the world cannot guarantee you good relationships. Iracebeth and little sister Mirana have followed very different paths in life, but as Alice discovers, the line between "good" and "bad" is blurred. There is more to their relationship than meets the eye.

Oversized head started growing after an accident on Fell Day.

Brace squeezes vegetable to shrink it.

This poor shrunken turnip is the latest victim of Iracebeth's hobby of torturing vegetables. Her gruesome pastime combines her love of cruelty and her love of teeny tiny things.

Chronosphere is pronounced "cronysphere" by Iracebeth.

Since being dethroned, Iracebeth no longer has the right to place her tiny crown on her huge head, but she still carries an ornamental sceptre.

The Red Queen

Nothing can excuse Iracebeth's murderous tendencies. However, as Alice finds out, on Fell Day, Iracebeth was the one who was wronged. Furthermore, the event caused her to trip and hit her head. She has never got over her little sister's betrayal and has been seeking revenge ever since.

The White Queen

Mirana is used to being adored by everyone – even once by her sister "Racie". But this gentle, fair-tempered queen is hiding a terrible secret. As a child she betrayed her sister. It was a seemingly minor incident, but Iracebeth never forgot what her supposedly kind sister did – and Underland has suffered as a result.

Mirana's crown is another source of sibling rivalry. King Oleron, concerned by Iracebeth's temper, passed the crown to her younger sister. Spoilt and petulant Iracebeth has never forgiven this act.

Sisterly Betrayal

Queen Elsemere believed Mirana over Iracebeth when they were children. On Fell Day, Mirana stole the last jam tart and lied about it, blaming her sister. She even planted the crumbs under Racie's bed.

"I ATE THE TARTS AND I LIED ABOUT IT... PLEASE FORGIVE ME."

Mirana has never forgiven herself for causing Racie's accident. She confesses her guilt when challenged by her sister, but is this heart-to-heart enough to lay sisterly rivalries to rest?

91

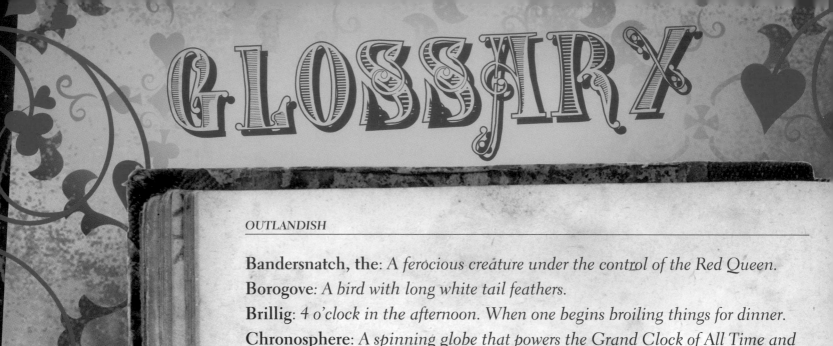

GLOSSARY

OUTLANDISH

Bandersnatch, the: *A ferocious creature under the control of the Red Queen.*

Borogove: *A bird with long white tail feathers.*

Brillig: *4 o'clock in the afternoon. When one begins broiling things for dinner.*

Chronosphere: *A spinning globe that powers the Grand Clock of All Time and can be used as a time machine.*

Crims: *The central area of Underland. It is here that the Talking Flowers grow.*

Downal wyth Bluddy Behg Hid: *Down with the Red Queen; Underland Underground Resistance slogan.*

Ezel: *High, go higher, go up.*

Fairfarren: *Farewell; may you travel far under fair skies.*

Faldinal: *The day Absolem ordered the Vorpal Sword to be forged.*

Fell Day: *The day Princess Mirana stole the last jam tart and betrayed her sister, Iracebeth, who then fell and hit her head.*

Frabjous Day: *The day Alice slays the Jabberwocky and frees Underland from the oppression of the Red Queen.*

Frumious: *Dirty and smelly.*

Fustilug: *The day after Shatterky when the Red Queen enslaved the free animals in her palace and forced them to act as furniture, ornaments or sports equipment.*

Futterwacken: *The Underlanders' dance of unbridled joy.*

Gallymoggers: *Crazy.*

Gleb: *The day the sky rained fish for no apparent reason.*

Griblig Day: *The day Alice will return to Underland.*

Gummer Slough: *Dangerous swamp of thick, viscous mud.*

Horunvendush Day: *The day the Red Queen took control of Underland.*

Jabberwocky: *A deadly creature employed as the Red Queen's ultimate weapon.*

Jubjub bird: *A bird under the control of the Red Queen.*

Keltikidik: *In celebration of the White Queen; a day when everyone in Underland wore only white, drank only milk and if they had to tell lies, they could only be white ones.*

Klotchyn: *"Heads up" or "Pay attention".*

Marmoreal: *The location of the White Queen's castle.*

Naught for usal: *It's no use trying.*

Nunz: *"Wait" or "Don't go; not now".*

Oraculum: *The Calendar of all the days of Underland since the Beginning. Each day has its own title and illustration.*

Orgal: *To the left.*

Outlands: *The untamed land to the west of Witzend.*

Outlandish: *The old language spoken in the Outlands; used by the Underland Underground Resistance as a code in the revolution against the Red Queen.*

Pishalver: *A vile-tasting potion that makes one shrink.*

Queast: *A land to the east, but "not in the least".*

Quillian: *The following day after Alice returns.*

Saganistute: *A wise person of poetry and vision.*

Salazen Grum: *A port city where the Red Queen lives.*

Shatterky: *The day the White Queen was banished to Marmoreal.*

Shunder: *The first morning that the sun rose on Underland.*

Slurvish: *Selfish or self-centred.*

Snud: *A region in the south of Underland.*

Stang: *To the right.*

Toomalie Day: *The celebration day for the coming of age of Princess Mirana and the crowning of the heir to the throne.*

Tulgey Wood: *Where Alice meets the Jabberwocky.*

Underland: *The real name for the place Alice calls "Wonderland".*

Upelkuchen: *A cake that makes one grow.*

Witzend: *The western land where the Hatter and the Cheshire Cat were born.*

Yadder: *Far away; "Way yadder beyond the Crossling in Snud."*

Zounder: *A warning to "Look out behind you!"*

Curious Language

When Alice hears Outlandish being spoken for the first time, she is very confused. The words sound familiar to her but they are not quite right – a bit like Underland itself.

INDEX

DK | Penguin Random House

Editorial Assistant Lauren Nesworthy
Senior Editor Elizabeth Dowsett
Senior Designers Owen Bennett, Anna Formanek, Lynne Moulding
Pre-production Producer Siu Yin Chan
Producer Zara Markland
Managing Editor Sadie Smith
Design Manager Ron Stobbart
Publisher Julie Ferris
Art Director Lisa Lanzarini
Publishing Director Simon Beecroft

First published in Great Britain in 2016 by
Dorling Kindersley Limited
80 Strand, London, WC2R 0RL
A Penguin Random House Company

10 9 8 7 6 5 4 3 2 1
001–294393–05/16

Page design copyright © 2016 Dorling Kindersley Limited

Some content previously published in 2010
in Great Britain as *Alice in Wonderland: The Visual Guide*.

Alice in Wonderland
Based on the classic story by Lewis Carroll
Based on the screenplay by Linda Woolverton
Produced by Richard D. Zanuck, Joe Roth,
Suzanne Todd and Jennifer Todd
Directed by Tim Burton

Alice Through the Looking Glass
Based on the classic story by Lewis Carroll
Based on the screenplay by Linda Woolverton
Directed by James Bobin

A CIP catalogue record for this book is available from the British Library.

ISBN: 978–0-24125-628-2

Printed in Italy.

DK would like to thank Chelsea Alon, Ashley Leonard,
Rachel Alor and Dale Kennedy at Disney.

A WORLD OF IDEAS:
SEE ALL THERE IS TO KNOW

Discover more at
www.dk.com